HOW 2 VEND AND

WIN!

at Venice Beach

by Tony B. Conscious
(The Ghetto Van-Go)

How 2 VEND and WIN at Venice Beach

Cover Design by: Nic The Artist

Published by: TONY B. CONSCIOUS for

CONSCIOUS ENTERPRISES

First Printing: 2011

ISBN: 978-0-98-28091-3-6

Printed in the **UNITED STATES OF AMERICA**

Special Thanks to BILL ROSENDAHL
(11 TH DISTRICT COUNCILMAN)
WHO MADE FREE SPEECH ZONE OF
VENICE BEACH BOARDWALK INTO THE
WORLD'S LARGEST SWAPMEET!

TABLE OF CONTENTS

INTRO

When I first wrote *"Life's A Beach and Then You Die"*, I would receive a lot of questions on the whole starving artist", How does one survive on Venice" topic. I would get these types of questions twittered, emailed, Facebooked and text messaged daily and almost to the point of complete shock. I couldn't believe that there were that many people who just did not know or who were desperate enough to want to hustle at *Venice Beach*. Then, I took a moment and thought about *Los Angeles County* alone, then *Southern California*, the State and then America. I asked myself the honest questions: how many people are unemployed, retired and/or disabled but talented, witty, intelligent, intellectual, crafty, and self-motivated to actually take advantage of an opportunity when it's presented to them? Well, quite a few. So, after a little research and a lot of thought, I decided that there was a wide open market for a book of this caliber.

As the saying goes, *"Necessity is the mother of invention"*. And applying that to Venice Beach, another saying came to my mind as well, *"opportunity is simply a port to unity"*. So with these two quotes floating around in my head and a desire to create a product that would basically **sell itself**, I picked up the pen to write this book.

I have found that *some of these principles and concepts, strategies and "hustles" can be applied in almost any city, state or country,* while others, unfortunately are very limited to Venice Beach only.

Please read the book, *apply it* when and if needed and like my comrade *"Stic Man"* from the Hip-Hop group, **"Dead Prez"** would say, *"Pimp the system, don't let the system pimp you..."*

THE HISTORY OF VENDING ON THE BOARDWALK

In the 1890's when **Abbot Kinney** founded (or created) the "Venice Beach" area (as we now know it), he dreamed of it being reminiscent of **Venice, Italy**. However, it wasn't until Abbot Kinney died (1920) and the City of Los Angeles demolished or converted most of his attractions or amusements into one long beach without canals nor rides, did even the thought of vending even come into play.

The once conservative, segregated, Disney-land type place that we all now know as Venice didn't become the *"free speech vending zone"* many of us are accustomed to until the 1960's and 70's.

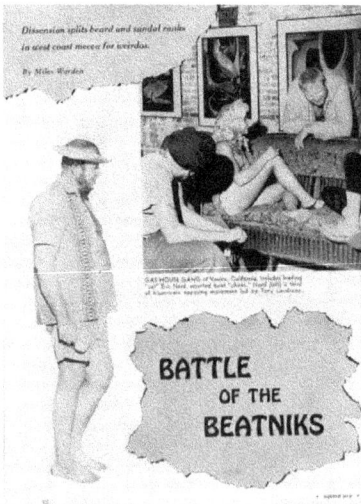

In the 60's, the ~~beats"~~ or ~~beatniks"~~ came into Venice bringing with them a Bohemian lifestyle. Their lifestyles were centered around poetry, jazz and art.

They would hang on the beaches and in the coffee houses and laid the foundations for the Venice Beach that so many know and love today.

The Beatniks set the stage for the Hippies to come to Venice and just have a field day". They had pot parties", would roller-skate, hula hoop and by 1976 Venice had become not only the Roller-skating capital of the world" but the free-speech hub of America.

Artists, painters, mimes, jugglers and musicians all flocked to the Venice Boardwalk to express themselves under the First Amendment, Free Expression Zone" policy adopted by the City of Venice in the late 60's and early 70's. It wasn't until the mid-60's and early 70's that Venice actually became a tourist attraction again

almost 50 years after the demise of Abbot Kinney and his coastline vision. With the rise of the "Beatniks" and then the

"Hippies", entrepreneurs started seeing financial potential of Venice and immediately started building, renting, leasing, and selling novelties and souvenirs out of the Venice Ocean Front Walk storefronts. These stores were located on the east side of the Front Walk or "Boardwalk" as it is commonly referred to as.

The Westside was reserved for "artists and expressionists". This was a practice commonly known not just in Venice but all around the world.

However in the early 80's, as financial times got a little harder, more and more people found Venice to be an excellent alternative to working temporary jobs and a viable solution to the "starving artist syndrome".

So, more and more people started utilizing the Boardwalk as an employment opportunity and a flea market as opposed to a soapbox or a world stage.

By the late eighties, of the Boardwalk artists, economic opportunists and other occupants had become very territorial. You either had to pay someone, know someone or fight somebody to get a space on the Boardwalk. There were altercations daily oftentimes leading to fistfights and even stabbings. Nepotism and narcissism had become the standard and the norm instead of the exception.

As a consequence, when the nineties came in; Venice started working on getting everything on the Boardwalk back to the way it was originally intended. The Free Speech laws were revisited and certain elements and items were either discouraged and/or banned from the Boardwalk by the Venice Neighborhood Council and the Parks and Recreation Department. As the battle ensued, the artists, musicians and the City stayed in a tug of war.

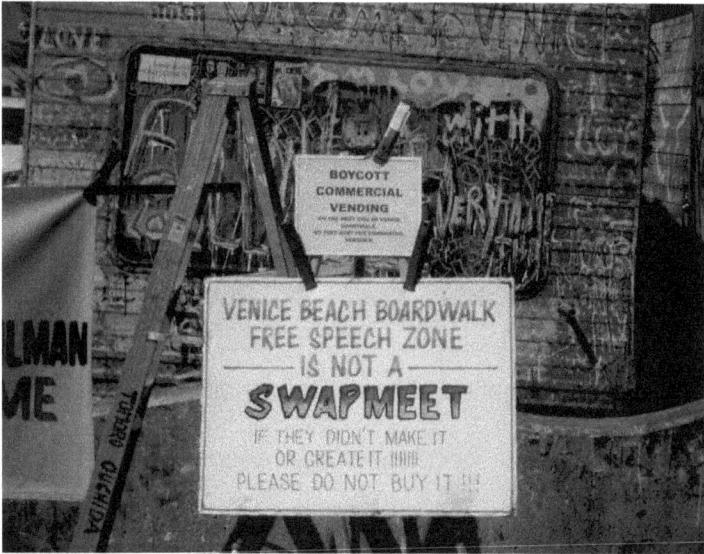

Unfortunately, in 1996 the City finally won. The City of Los Angeles along with the Department of Parks and Recreation had created a lottery system that was unconstitutional, prejudiced and culturally biased. It was immediately posted, implemented and enforced, violating several vendors, artists, and musicians' civil rights. It was challenged, taken to court, thrown out and then re-written several times.

A lottery system for distribution of the space on the Boardwalk was another element that was added. With it came a ―permit system" that allowed the City to make revenue off of charging people a nominal fee to practice their 1st Amendment Rights.

Of course this too was struck down by the courts, leading to all sorts of lawsuits that have been thrown out, are currently pending and even a few with out of court, cash settlements.

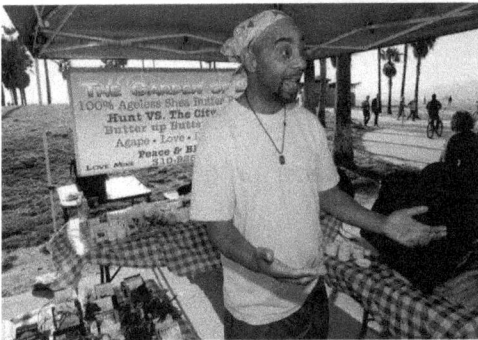

Just recently, one vendor by the name of Michael Hunt, after years of fighting for his rights, finally received the court's blessing and was awarded a nice six figures for all of the harassment and false imprisonment he received due to the ordinances.

That was the straw that broke the ordinances back or so to speak. Now, at least temporarily, it is completely a free for all.

Anybody and everybody who has anything to sell is trying their hand at vending on the Boardwalk.

At first, you could only sell things you had made by hand. But now you can sell anything you get into a space, on a cart or carry in your hands.

Yes, it is a long way away from Abbot Kinney's vision, but it still is better and a lot easier to make a decent honest dollar than anywhere else in the world.

WHY VEND AT VENICE?

If you have turned on the television, talked to your parents, friends, coworkers or even the common everyday person on the street you probably have heard the same thing come out of their mouths. *"Unemployment is up, the economy is bad, it's really hard to make a dollar and times are tough."* Whether you've personally experienced this or not, this is the reality going around. A great deal of layoffs, mortgage crisis issues, corporate takeovers, oil price hikes and natural disasters have led some to be literally down and out" with no ways nor means.

And then, **there's a light at the end of the tunnel**. For those who don't want to do anything illegal (or perceived as such) there's only one place you can make a viable amount of revenue every single day without punching a clock, paying a booth or stall fee nor having to answer to anybody: This place is **Venice Beach**.

This is one of the top tourist spots in the whole country and the *only one* that **millions upon millions come to annually and spend hundreds of thousands of dollars on art and other collectible souvenirs created and/or sold to them by street**

artists and musicians. You can create and sell almost anything without having to report it nor pay taxes to the I.R.S. As a matter of fact, **most of the artists, performers, vendors and even the homeless are on E.B.T. (food stamps), welfare and/or are living in Section 8 housing due to their "untraceable" incomes.** Another beautiful thing about Venice is the flexibility. What most go through just to make a dollar is incredible in the *"corporate and blue collar—*world. However, at Venice, all you have to do is show up at the right place at the right time and you're bound to make more in one day then some make in a whole week.

The levels of *discrimination* and *harassment* by management and coworkers, oftentimes drive some to an *insane* state of mind and even leads a few to become *"postal".* At Venice, you can work when you want, how you want, where you want, if you want. This is all up to you.

Another benefit of being at **Venice** is the maximum exposure that you receive on a daily basis. This also leads to the most promising opportunities (*monetarily lucrative* and otherwise).

A prime example of this is the mere fact that *Hollywood* productions (such as the television show *"Californication"*) are always shooting on the Boardwalk. They are additionally always using the *"locals"* and *Venice artists, vendors and patrons* as *"atmosphere"*. **They constantly look for interesting faces, personalities and performances to feature, discover, highlight and introduce to the industry.** Many people have gone from nobody to somebody just by being on the Boardwalk at the right time.

Jim Morrison was a poet who used to be a Beatnik poet on the Boardwalk and later became the lead singer for the internationally acclaimed, multi-platinum award winning rock group, The Doors".

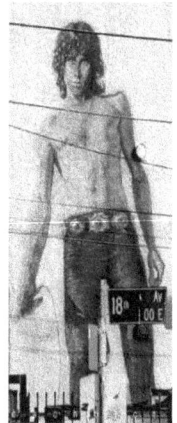

Another well-known Venice Beach icon (who happens to be alive) is the one and only Harry Perry. He has been in over 100 films and television productions. He is a living testament to the power of the Boardwalk and its exposure.

The third and equally notable person is Michael Colyar. He is known as the official "Venice Beach Comedian". He has the best success story out of anyone on the Boardwalk. He came from the streets of Chicago to the sands of Venice Beach where he'd do five one-hour shows per day, until he became "discovered". He then went on to host B.E.T's "Live From L.A." and "The Big Black Comedy Show".

In 1990, he won $100,000 as the Grand Champion of Comedy on "Star Search" and donated half of the money to homeless charities and then was honored in December of 2000 by the City of Venice by placing his handprints, shoeprints and tip jar in the cement. He has been in over 40 major motion pictures and television shows and is still going and going and going.

There's also a common practice by the production companies called a ‑buy-out" on the Boardwalk. This happens when a particular performer, artist, vendor, or person is occupying a space that the director needs or needs to be blank (or silent) for a shot or scene. The production assistant is instructed to negotiate with the occupier or ‑buy them out" of the designated space. The production usually pays $200-$500 for the spot, depending on how good of a negotiator the recipient is. There are some Venice Beach regulars who stake out these spots days and weeks before the designated day(s) of shooting. So, ironically, you could set up in a spot and make $200-$500 within 15 minutes of the whole day and go home or away with a smile just for being at the right place at the right time.

THE GOOD

To give it to you as easily as possible, I'll tell you all the advantages in a short list.

1. **Tax-Free Money:** Everything under the table, no bosses, nor I.R.S. taxes, no booth fees.

2. **Perfect Weather and**

   Environment: You can go swimming or jogging in the morning, make money in afternoon and then watch the sunset in the evening. The temperature (even in the winter) is seldom beneath 65-70 degrees. Most days (even on Christmas) it's normally hot and sunny.

3. **Flexibility and Freedom:** You can wear what you want, say what you want, think what you want and sell what you want. You can sing, dance, jump around, act cool or act a fool and the people around you will probably pay you no mind, while the tourists and Venice patrons might actually dig it and you may stumble upon a lucrative way to express yourself.

4. **Exposure:** *You will generally see 5,000 to 15,000 people a day pass you.* Not only are you seeing them, they are also seeing you. And that's not to mention all of the celebrities, athletes, special events media and production companies who film there as well. Most companies pay thousands of dollars for things (exposure) you can obtain for free.

5. **Memorable Experiences:** If you are a people person, you will have some of the sweetest times and memories, interacting

with different folks from all over the world. People have been known to meet their soul mates, future husbands, wives, lovers and best friends on the Boardwalk. Others have met their business partners and have been responsible for creating multi-million dollar companies in which the products were test marketed right on the Boardwalk.

THE BAD

Though being on the Venice Boardwalk as a vendor has its advantages, there are certain disadvantages as well. This is a list that you might want to consider.

1. **No Guaranteed Paycheck**: Fortunately, Venice Beach's Boardwalk offers nothing concrete nor absolute: Everyday is a different opportunity to create abundance and wealth, however you could leave with $1,000 one day and the next, not make a dime. It is a gamble, but some need a guarantee. Some need what they call stability". Venice Beach is for the most part stable in the fact that there won't be any chance of an act of nature" nor a calamity taking it away. However, the very thing that's in" today maybe out" tomorrow so it's a 50/50 chance situation.

2. **No Benefits**: Venice Beach offers no healthcare plan. Some work jobs simply for the medical and dental benefits. There's no sick leave on days you don't feel like working, no retirement pension, Medicare, nor vacation pay. You have a hard days work, for a hard day's pay, period.

3. **It's a Small Town/Tiny Community:** If you've ever lived in a small town, then you probably know what I'm talking about. When something or someone happens, everybody knows about it. There's a whole lot of gossipers, backstabbers and people who just have nothing better to do than to be up in another person's business. So, anything that happens, it's on the Boardwalk's topic list immediately. Words travel fast.

4. **The Early Bird Gets the Worm:** Unless you are willing to spend the night or get up at 3:00 AM in the morning (on the weekends), you are not guaranteed a spot on the boardwalk. Unemployment and competition has made the Boardwalk a -survival of the fittest" type of place. So, unless you are willing to lose a lot of sleep and dedicate your life to vending, you probably won't stand a chance of keeping a spot.

THE UGLY

1. **No Clean Bathrooms:** Unfortunately, one of the worst parts about being a vendor on the Boardwalk is the public bathrooms.

2. Not only are they already (when perfectly clean) dark and moist

inside, they also are frequently tagged, trashed and terrorized by the raunchiest, sleaziest, shadiest individuals who either live at and on the Beach or are regulars at Venice. If you are going to come to Venice, it's best to have gloves, anti-bacterial soap and napkins/toilet tissue with you at all times. Clean bathrooms are not a guarantee, and during the summer, the lines for them are so long, you have to have an additional person at your booth but that's a whole _nother issue within itself.

3. **Homeless/Dangerous Environment**: As just stated near the end of the last paragraph, it is an excellent idea to have an additional person with you who can help out and watch your back. *There are times (especially right around sunset) when the "natives get restless",* the crowds get hostile and the homeless get drunk. This is when it gets dangerous for the vendors. The crowds get too thick and fights erupt, things get smashed, stolen, or knocked over and out of desperation a lot of opportunists look for any opportunity to become opportunistic.

What that means is that *yes there are a lot of great people, artists, vendors, musicians and even homeless with good hearts.* But on the flipside of that coin is the fact *a lot of gangbangers, drug dealers, habitual alcohol and drug addicts and mentally unstable folks who have serious problems and no where to go frequent the beach as well.* So you've got to pick a spot and/or a block where the energy or vibe matches yours.

4. **L.A.P.D.** **Ticketing / Harassment:** Now the L.A.P.D.

at Venice can be one of two things to you, your friend or your foe.
It all depends on the way you present yourself, what you're selling
and what you're doing. Never be afraid to stop a police officer and
ask them questions about the laws, ordinances and Boardwalk
rules. Most of them will be glad to help you.

However, here's the sticky part; **not every cop enforces the
laws the same way**. Some operate and enforce based on the
-spirit" of the law(s). While others they follow each and every
letter of the law.

The reason I'm saying this is so that if you do decide to come
to Venice to vend or otherwise, you will know that you have to
watch what you do and how you do it.

*Parking tickets are up to $88 and fines for vendors can go
up to $200 or $300 dollars.* That's not to mention *smoking on*

the grass, open container and *riding your bike on the Boardwalk.* Some days the cops are cool, but on others, they have quotas or just want to impress their superiors. It's a risk we all take, but hey, the rewards are sometimes well worth the gambles.

Getting Started

Now that you've finally decided that you're going to try your luck (or tempt your fate) at Venice, there's a few things that you're going to need:

1. **A Good Pair of Walking /Jogging Shoes:**

Depending on what you decided to do, you could possibly be standing/or walking for 3 to 5 hours minimum.

2. **Comfortable Clothing:**

Venice is a very beautiful place and in the day it gets real hot and in the night it's a lot cooler. Sometimes the weather changes at the drop of a dime, or almost in a blink of an eye. So make sure you bring a light jacket as well.

3. **A Light, Portable, Table(s):**

Depending on what you're selling and how you intend to display it, you should definitely invest in some lightweight aluminum or plastic card or picnic tables. They are normally found in the outdoor/sporting goods department of most stores and run between $15-25 dollars. Most of them weigh between 7-10 lbs and are easy to carry. They are an invaluable part of vending, not just for Venice, but for anywhere you are. If you ever need to set something up, it's like…"BAM!!!"

4. "Easy Up"/Fold Down Tent & Umbrella:

5. One of the major necessities (besides a table) is something that can block the sun. There are a load of people who got heat exhaustion and pass out from sunstroke. So, having a tent, umbrella or some kind of cover is not only good for your health, it also makes the booth look and feel more professional. Oftentimes, it gets so hot on the Boardwalk, passerby's will only stop at booths where they can get a little bit of shade. It's a win-win situation on all levels...

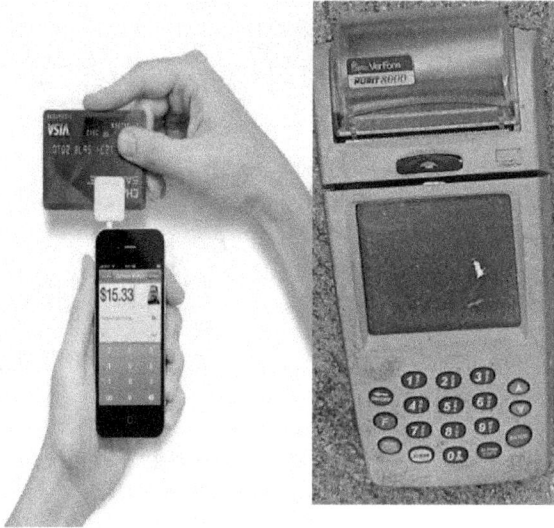

6. **A Credit Card Machine or the Square Application for Accepting Plastic**: In a time when everything in our society is going high tech and globally cash less, it is not only smart but also easy to make sure that people can give you money in a way that is easy and convenient for them.

7. **Music:** One of the most important things you can do for yourself is bring some music, a radio, or even an instrument with you. **With music, you not only are able to create a vibe or "the vibe" of your booth, it also makes the day fly by much faster.** Thousands of people will walk by you daily and just like in a department store, _a song can make them stop at your booth, stand not only to hear the tune, sing a long, appreciate it or reminisce, it also makes them want to look and see what else you have going on._ *A great deal of visual artists tend to use "Jazz" as the soundtrack to their art for it creates a "gallery" type atmosphere.* However, it all depends on what you're selling. Rock-n-Roll (Jimi Hendrix), Reggae (Bob Marley) or even Hip-Hop (Old School) may work depending on the energy or scene you're trying to set. *Live music always works* as well because then you

have (2) things going for you. One, is the fact, due to the rising economic desperation amongst people, there are more vendors than performers on the Boardwalk, yet there are tons of people who love to see and even come to see the live performances. And if you're halfway decent and have a tip jar you'll be generously rewarded by those who appreciate your music. So, that's double the income from the stuff you sell plus tips. The second is that it creates a festive atmosphere and people who see others engaged in an activity like to be "tag a longs". One person will attract two more, then those three will make three more stop and before you know it, you've got a crowd. And when you have a crowd, you have people of all walks of life from different places with various needs who might not normally see your merchandise or products who now are there for an extended amount of time and have nothing better do but check it out. It's another win, win situation.

8. **A CART / WAGON:**

Now after acquiring all these things (plus the merchandise) for your booth, you are going

to have a ton of stuff to get to the boardwalk. One of the essentials to walking up and down the boardwalk, searching for a spot or just getting everything light and heavy to the same place at the same time is a cart. Some use wagons, dollies, and even skateboards. The latter doesn't hold much, but a good dolly could get (2) booths worth of fixings to one area if you get a good one.

TOP 10 HUSTLES

Now, say you've decided to finally make that move to Venice Beach. You get there without a thin dime in your pocket and want to get your hustle on". These are the things you can do to go from nothing to something in a matter of days or maybe a week.

1. *Fly A Sign*

2. *Become a Vendor's Helper*

3. *Pizza Sign Holder*

4. *Recycle Cans*

5. *Broken Skateboard Decks*

6. *Alley Search/Dumpster Dive*

7. *Selling EBT/Food Stamps*

8. *Become Medical Marijuana Scout*

9. *Wash Cars*

10. *Performance:Sing/Dance/TellJokes*

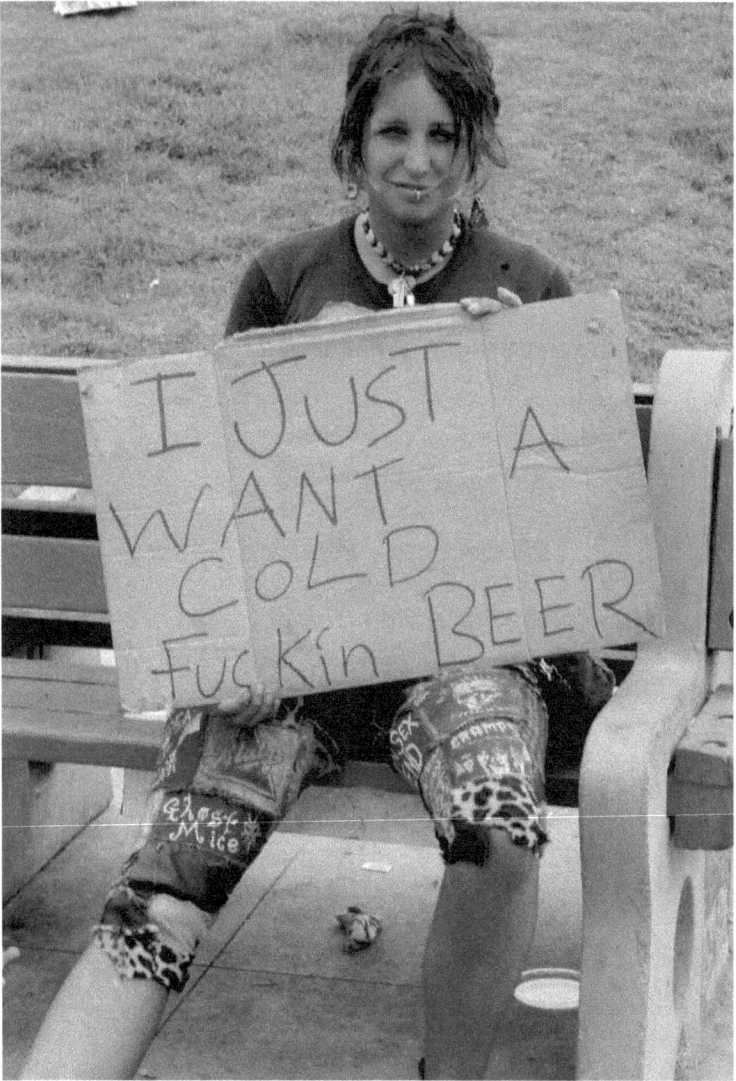

FLY A SIGN

The number one way to go from nothing to something on the Boardwalk is to simply ask for money in a stupid, crazy, silly, ignorant or outrageous way. Some "panhandlers" or "sign flyers" make more money than some who vend on the Boardwalk. All you have to do is think up an outrageous message or service. Some creative and very lucrative ones are:

- *"Shitty Advice" $100*

- *"Why lie? I need a beer"*

- *"I will work for marijuana"*

- *"Obama not the only one who needs change"*

- *"Out of work Supermodel"*

- *"One dollar short of a six pack"*

- *"Kick me in the nuts for $5.00"*

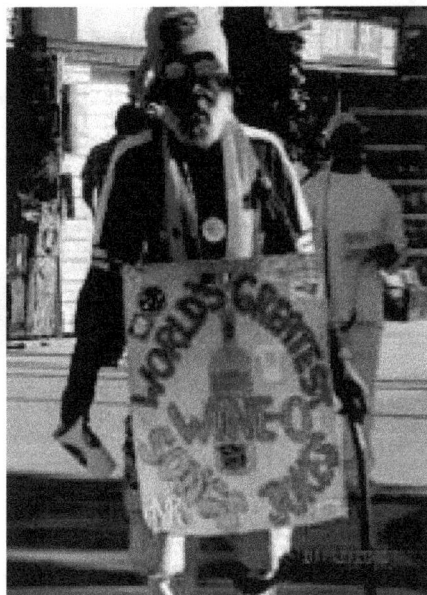

Now my favorite is a guy called the **"World's Greatest Wino"**. He told me once that he purposely comes with zero dollars on him, so he'll work his butt off taking pictures with folks or making people laugh which amounts to a whole lot of tips.

Some people (locals but tourists especially) love to take pictures with outrageous Venice Beach folks. If they like your sign and want to take a photo with it, tell em you require a donation. If enough people like it, you could walk away with a jar full of money just like that. Easy money for an easy sign. Go to the alley, get some cardboard, borrow a Sharpie"/ink pen from a vendor and you're set.

CUSTOM BUM SIGNS = PAY A LITTLE,

MAKE A LOT !!!

BECOME A VENDOR'S HELPER

On any given day, there are approximately 200 to 300 vendors on Boardwalk, trying to set-up stands, displays and booths of all shapes and sizes. Some carry their belongings and merchandise on carts from their cars, while others have storage lockers on the beach where they hold their goods. A great deal of them require a little assistance along the way to and from their destination, and most are willing to pay a helping hand what they are worth.

The average artist/vendor will pay a helper between $5-10 dollars for a little -muscle" or an extra body to carry the little or big things. Additionally, almost a third of all the vendors on the Boardwalk are women.

So, if you figure a person, realistically speaking is not going to be able to service all (200) vendors. But maybe (10), if he or she really works hard. So (10) ten times $5 to $10 dollars is equal to around $50 to $100 bucks in the morning alone. It's double that if the person goes back to help these same vendors at the end of the day when the sun is setting. And what's even greater is the job security in it. So many people come through Venice (homeless or otherwise) that vendors have to hold on to those who are consistent, dependable and trustworthy. Good help is really hard to find (and keep).

They say it's the early bird who catches the worm, and at Venice if you're serious, focused and a hard worker, there are tons of worms to catch.

PIZZA SIGN HOLDER

There are very few places in the world where you go and have opportunities dropped in your lap daily. There are (2) major pizza franchises on the Boardwalk. One of them is *Big Daddy's Pizza* on the corner of Ocean Front Walk and Market Street. **The other (2) are Generic 99¢ and Pizza joints up near Westminster.** The thing that they have in common however is their dependence upon sign holders to attract customers to their businesses. The owners are willing to pay a person, any person, to hold a sign, engage folks and make them laugh, smile and buy some pizza. **Now Big Daddy's owner (Larry Parker) is known for always treating his employees fairly, the sign holders included.** When I last checked, he was paying a **flat $5 an hour** rate. As for **the owner of the other (2) shops**, there are several different stories. *He tends to pay $10-25 dollars a day, (which could be from 5-9 hours) and give the person some pizza and coke.* If you're new to town, or down on your luck, however, it's better than nothing.

RECYCLE CANS

Now on Venice Beach, there are approximately 100 garbage cans scattered and spaced throughout the Boardwalk area. There are restaurants, pizza shops and a few grocery stores as well where drinking sodas are as normal for people as breathing air. The trash cans fill up quite quickly as thousands of people rush to get a cold drink and then discard its containers in an equally accelerated fashion.

Thousands of people, hundreds of soda cans and bottles and tons of garbage cans makes for a big window of opportunity. If you've got the drive, you can turn this into a literal -cash cow".

BROKEN SKATEBOARD DECKS

In a trend started originally by Tony B. Conscious ―The Ghetto Van-Go", quite a few Venice Beach artists have embarked on a ―going green" project that includes (but is not limited to) taking broken skateboards and turning them into art.

With the Venice Skate Park hosting hundreds of skateboarders daily and (2) skate shops within a 4 block radius of Venice, it would be almost as easy as collecting recyclable bottles and cans to go to the shops and park and collect broken boards. *Tony B. and other artists pay between $2-5 dollars per board,* so you definitely will earn every cent you deserve.

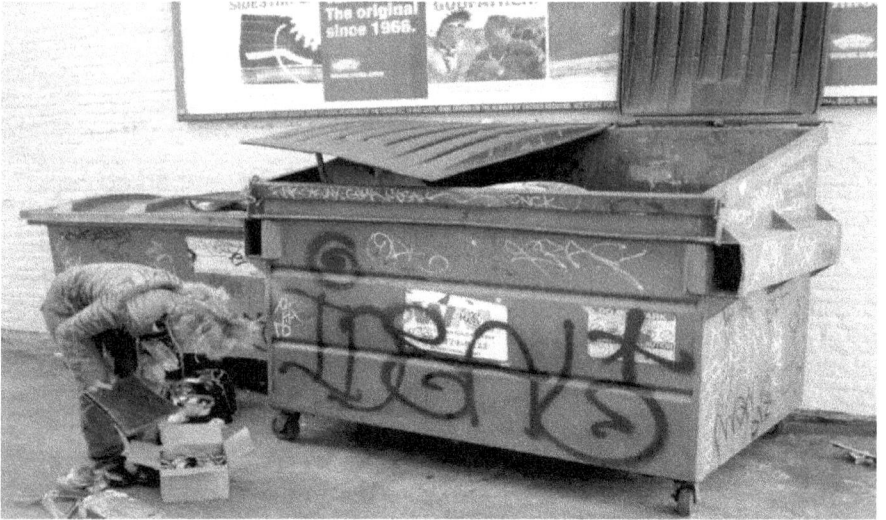

ALLEY SEARCH/DUMPSTER DIVE

—Oa man's trash, is another man's treasure" is the statement that best describes America's obsession with swap-meets, yard sales and even Venice Beach's Boardwalk. If you walk down the alleys and check the side streets, you will find all kinds of trinkets, collectables and unique odds and ends that people just do not have a use for anymore. From boxes of books (that can be sold on the Boardwalk for $1 a piece) to picture and futon frames (that can be sold for cheap to vendors) can be found on any given day and instantly converted to cash. The deeper you (dumpster) dive, the more you'll survive.

Some people will do anything for cash. Some people will do anything for food. Some people will trade one for the other at the drop of a hat. Venice is one of the only places where everything is on sale. If you happen to be on "food stamps" (now electronically delivered) called EBT, you can easily convert those to cash with any of the vendors who have big families and will gladly help you out and fill up their refrigerator.

BECOME A MEDICAL MARIJUANA SCOUT

Now there's a thin line on the Boardwalk between what's legal and what's not. And now with the Medical Marijuana movement, the lines have not only been blurred and merged, sometimes they zigzag and intertwine like ropes dangling in the wind.

It is a proven fact and unlawful to sell marijuana unless you are in a dispensary in California.

There are thousands of people (guilty and innocent) who are incarcerated that will attest to that fact that Judges do not waiver on this law.

However, *what if a medical doctor or dispensary allowed individuals to be free agents and promote their businesses or offices and was willing to give you a lucrative finders' fee for each person you lead to them?* Well, that's another way in which people on the Boardwalk are making tons of money.

The "scouts" collect a "finders' fee" for each and every person they introduce and spends money on a medical card and/or some "medicine". You might earn some quick cash, a little -product", if you indulge, or a combination of both.

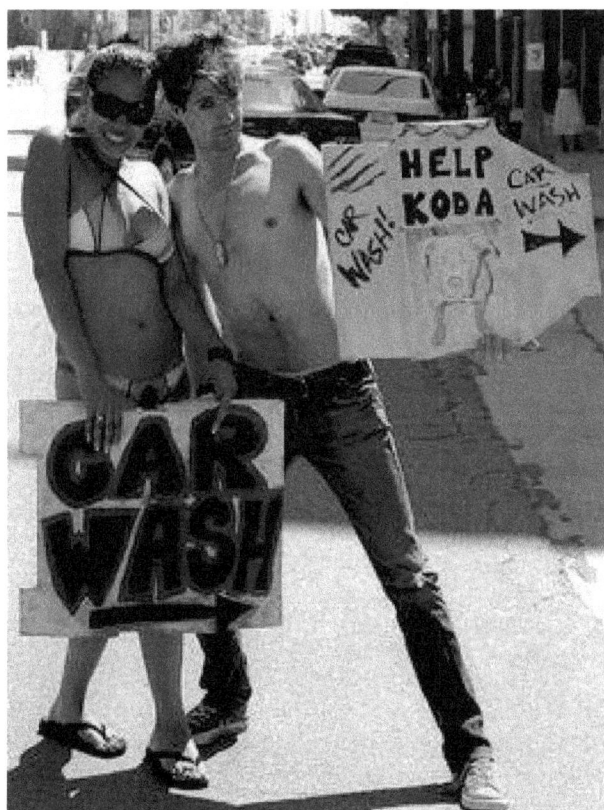

<u>WASH CARS</u>

With so many parking lots for the thousands of beachgoers coming daily to Venice, there has been a trend amongst transients, homeless and hustlers. The trend is to do whatever, whenever, wherever. As a result, some sit around with buckets and wash people's cars while they walk, shop and/or eat at a restaurant. All you need is a bucket, the beach has all the water you can possibly desire, and the portable bathrooms have soap dispensaries, so it's a no brainer. The only thing you might need is a rag, but I've actually seen folks take the shirt off of their own backs.

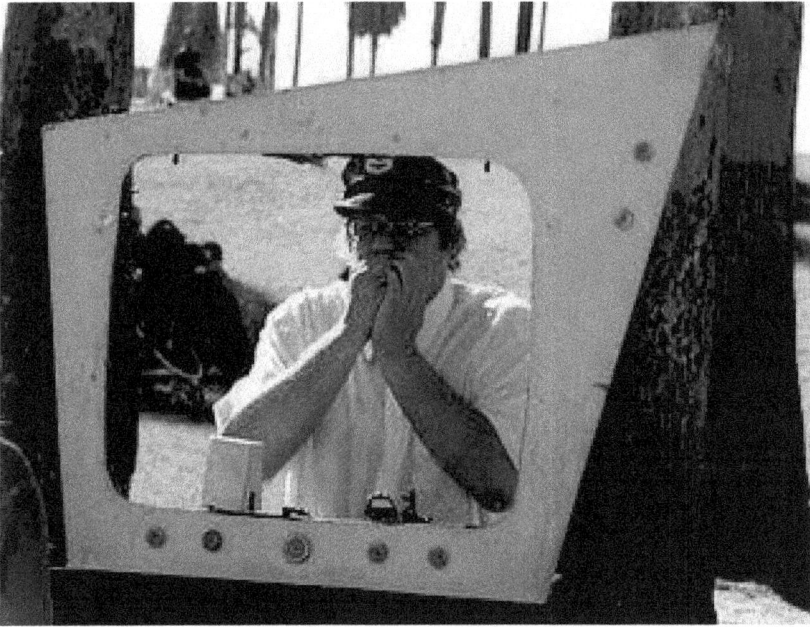

PERFORMANCES:

Sing Dance Tell Jokes

Now the best way to make a dollar on Venice is to just stand or walk around with a tip jar singing, telling jokes, reciting poetry or just performing anything. With the multitude of personalities, children and free-spirited types, you're bound to touch someone's spirit. And if and when you do, you will see your tip jar go from zero to lots of dinero in no time at all.

To sum this chapter up in a few words, I would say "Don't ever quit". At Venice Beach, as long as you can take control of your addictions and are willing to get up, work hard and focus, you can't lose. Venice is literally a pot of gold just sitting at the average everyday persons feet. People have come to Venice and went from nothing to property owners and/or celebrities just by hustling, working hard and saving. Then there are others, who make enough to support their abusive lifestyles and drink and smoke themselves to death. Which way you want to go, the opportunity awaits and the choice is yours.

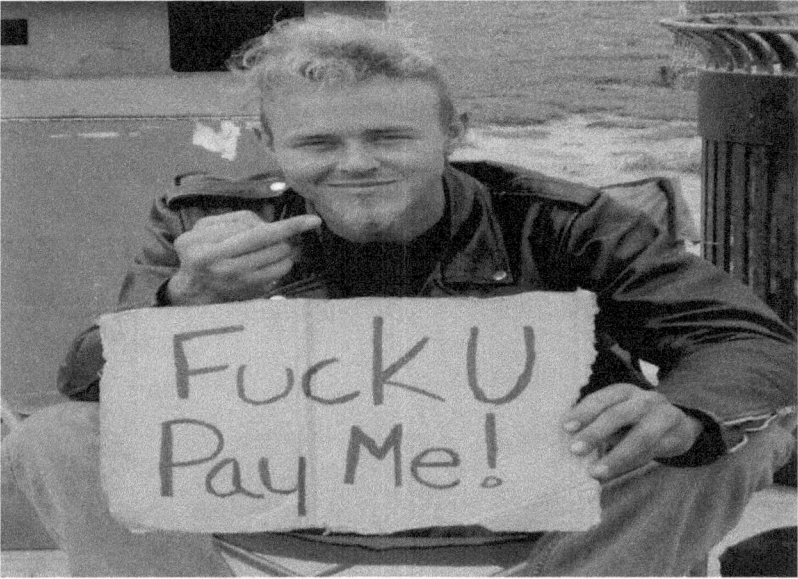

TOP 10 WAYS TO FLIP YOUR MONEY

Now if you have a little bit of money to invest in getting started, there are quite a few ways to **double or triple your money** and/or start a lasting business venture on Venice Beach.

Whether you just want to flip your money or make a steady income continuously, these are the top (10) ways to do so:

1.   *Selling Water/Beverages*

2.   *Selling Candy/Snacks*

3.   *Buying Wholesale Jewelry*

4.   *Incense/Oils*

5.   *Sage*

6.   *Rasta Anything*

7.   *Venice Beach Anything*

8.   *Downloaded Pictures*

9.   *Sports Teams Anything*

10.   *99¢ Store Anything...*

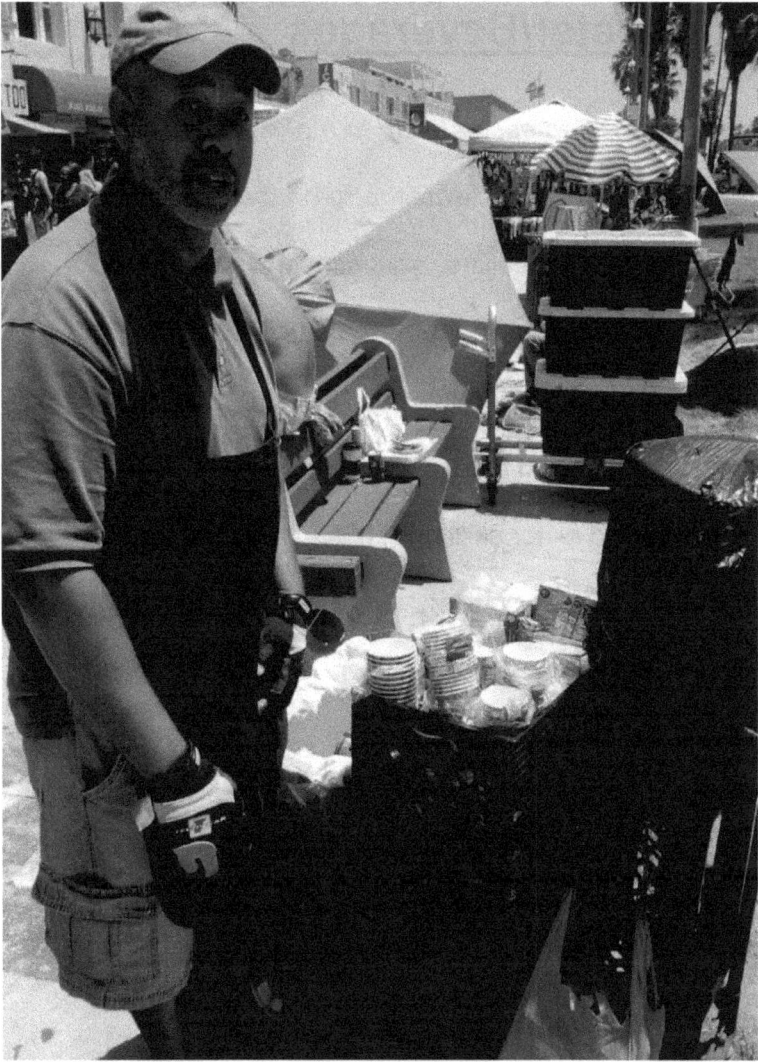

Selling Water/Beverages

The quickest and easiest way to make money on Venice is through selling bottled water and/or beverages. For an investment of $20-25 dollars, you can purchase a cooler with wheels that will hold at least 48-12 oz cans or bottles of water that when sold for a dollar or two will not only return you initial investment, but give you the revenue to stock up and do the same daily. With bottled water selling (in bulk) for as low as $3.99 for a 24 pack (of 16 oz bottles), *and Venice Beach attracting somewhere between one and ten thousand people daily (sometimes up to even 30,000)* there's no way you can lose.

Having a cooler not only provides a service for the vendors who can't leave their booths but also for those who refuse to pay for overpriced beverages and water that the restaurants, liquor stores and food vendors on the eastside of the Boardwalk display. It's an investment in which everybody wins, and you, simply cannot lose.

Selling Candy/Snacks

There's only one thing (besides water) that is a guaranteed "quick money flip" at Venice Beach, and that is candy and snacks. Years ago, it was an occasional Girl Scout cookie sale or a "Football Fundraiser" with a $1 dollar candy bar people would see every now and then. However, *at Venice, with so many tourists, locals and vendors who will relinquish a buck for darn near anything*, making money off of something so tempting and tasteful isn't rocket science. With **Costco** and other

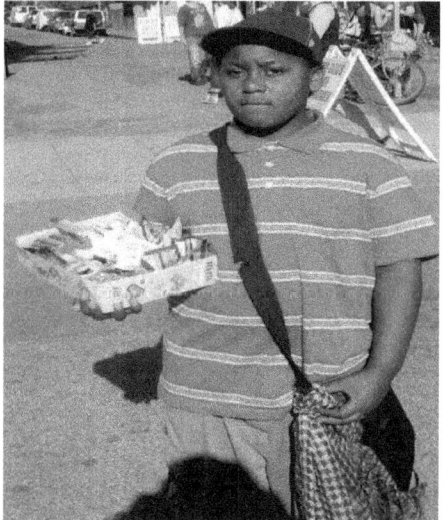

places like **Sam's Club** and **Smart and Final** selling everything in bulk (like Snickers for $6.99/36 pack), the possibilities are infinite. Like with beverages, get a big cooler, fill it up with goodies, chips and whatever else. Walk up and down the boardwalk and (minus your investment) you'll make more an hour than most construction workers do. Some say that *"if it don't make dollas, it don't make sense..."*. Well, this makes a whole lot of both. If you give people what they are addicted to, they'll give you what you need to get by. Sugar and salt are two legal drugs that people will never kick and will always be in style.

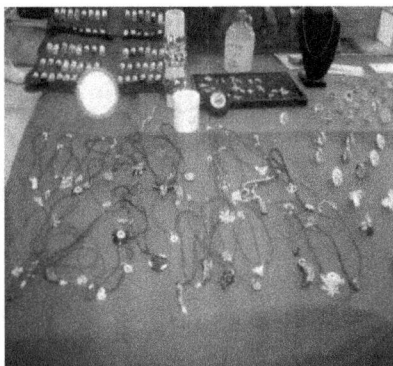

Buying wholesale jewelry

Now *approximately 75 percent of the vendors on Venice (on either side of the Boardwalk) are selling and make large profits off of jewelry (bracelets, necklaces, earrings and feather accessories).* Out of that 75 percent, only 20 percent actually make, create or manufacture the jewelry themselves. The others all buy everything from Venice Beach -Palm Tree" key chains to **Buddha necklaces** and even -Ohm" symbol **nose and belly button rings** from *Downtown LA's Wholesale District.*

If you have $100 to spend, you can get enough merchandise to turn a little investment into a thousand dollar profit. **Most rings, necklaces and other jewelry oriented merchandise sells for $6 per dozen, that's .50¢ each.** You can then charge, on the

Boardwalk from $2-5 per piece. Now you do the math on that!!! It doesn't matter how many college degrees you have or don't have, **even a 5th grader could see the profit in that.**

The most frequented booths (out of everything on the Boardwalk) are the jewelry tables, cause women love to shop and love to adorn themselves.

The City, the merchants, the artists and performers have all been trying to get rid of these "commercial booths",

but only time will tell if this will happen. In the meantime, you better get it, while the gettin' is good. An ordinance to ban wholesale jewelry is at least a few thousand dollars away.

Incense and Oils

The second most frequented booths on the Boardwalk are those that sell incense and body/burning oils. The oils (as far as Venice goes) go back to the Beatnik/Hippie era of the 60's and 70's and are one of the oldest staples of Venice. There are several places in the City where you can buy oils, incense sticks and cones, incense holders, burners, body oils, oil burners and bottles for the oils.

The two most popular are on Crenshaw between Vernon and Slauson. **The good thing about incense and oils are the**

fact that they are protected by the First Amendment (in case they ever change the ordinance), *you can walk around or have a booth with them* and they sell just as good (if not better than) jewelry and water. Just imagine the possibilities and if you like the smell of new fresh money, get some fresh and new oils and incense. These are (2) scents that blend perfectly together.

Sage

Now just like incense and oils, sage goes back to the late 60's and early 70's on the Boardwalk. It is also one of those things that goes back to indigenous cultures and is said *to remove all negative energy in the area when burned and the smoke is heavy and thick. The ancients believed sage symbolized wisdom, skill, esteem, long life, good health, domestic virtue, mitigation of grief and increased physic powers*.

However, with all that being said, *the best thing about sage is the fact that most of the time if you know where to look, you get pounds of it for free.*

It is completely of the earth, but ***unlike marijuana it's not illegal to grow***, so you can travel up to the **Malibu Canyons**, the **Santa Monica** and **Hollywood Hills, Pasadena, Altadena, Griffith Park** and quite a few other places and bring a big satchel full to the Boardwalk and sell it all day, week, month and year without have paid nothing for it!!! That's a 100% profit all the time and from simply hiking, enjoying nature and sharing it with others.

Rasta Anything

The one thing that has become the most marketable in America as well as worldwide is the color combination "red, gold and green". Even more than America's Red, White and Blue, if you have anything with the "Rasta colors" as they are called, you are guaranteed to sell out.

Originally linked to Bob Marley, Reggae a "One Love" for all mentality and marijuana, these colors for most are the hippest and always in style, trendiest that Venice Beach has to offer.

From little string/yarn bracelets, to necklaces, hats, wristbands, towels, t-shirts, and even shoestrings, it all goes fast.

Now the quickest way to get your hands on some of this ‑Rasta stuff" is by going to Downtown Los Angeles by the way of the (10) freeway (traveling eastbound) and getting off at the Main Street exit. There's a store called **"Rasta World"** from which you can retrieve everything you could ever think of in these colors (and so much more). You can acquire over a thousand dollars worth of merchandise for pennies on the dollar (as long as you don't mind that it's made in China). What a gold mine.

<u>Venice Beach Anything</u>

If there's one thing that is a no-brainer at Venice Beach, it is the mere fact that *all you have to do is find anything that has the words "Venice Beach, California" or "Venice Beach" on it and because of the high number of tourists, you will sell out immediately.* There are tons of stores who sell all kind of cool collectibles from skateboards, surfboards, clocks and keychains to the very Venice Beach hoodies, caps and t-shirts sold on the eastside by the merchants. **They are all located in Downtown Los Angeles (on Main, 4th, 5th and 6th streets)** and typically sell for between $6-36 per dozen depending on what item it is. Or...**you can make your own souvenirs and throw "Venice Beach", a Palm tree or anything California-ish on it**.

Buy or make a few stencils, some paint and you've got a year round business simply based on two words: Venice Beach.

Downloaded Pictures

Now one of the most profitable ways to make money on the Boardwalk are pictures, posters and artwork. There are more images sold on the Boardwalk than almost anything else you'll ever see. One out of every three people leave with some sort of original, downloaded, reproduced, or photocopied artwork or picture. Now about one-third of these images are original works done by visual and graphic artists who are on the Boardwalk using their skills and talents to make a living. **However, the other two-thirds of images sold are "creatively captured", cheaply commercialized or downloaded.**

The easiest way to make money off of images on the Boardwalk is to simply download them off of the Internet. If you have an Apple Computer you can use the *"drag and drop"* feature to pull it straight into photo or onto your desktop in a jpeg form. From there, you can use **Photoshop** or another program like **"Paint It"** to retouch, enhance or transform the images in any way, shape or form you desire. Once reconfiguration is complete (if desired), you can then reproduce the image(s) in 5x7, 8x10, 11x14, 16x20, 18x24 or even bigger poster sizes (depending on what you want to do with them and how you want to sell them). The most popular sizes are 5x7, 11x14, or full size posters.

All these sizes can be made conveniently right on the Boardwalk at the one and only print shop in Venice Beach, Dynamic Image. They do almost any size, shape, color, and paper weight fast, efficiently and inexpensively. You can then get plastic bags from a comic book store, or go to the 99¢ store and buy frames to put the prints in. Or, you can simply display (1) of each of the images and roll the rest up in individual tubular posters.

Now that you know the how, it's time to know the what...

1. *Marilyn Monroe*

2. Venice Beach Scenes

3. LA/Hollywood City Skylines

# 4.	*LA Lakers/Kobe*

5.   *Bob Marley*

6. *Jimi Hendrix*

7.   *N.W.A*

8.   *Tupac*

TUPAC SHAKUR
1971 - 1996

9.   *The Beatles*

10. Skull Faces

Now if all of these still aren't enough, go to Google and put in the search bar ─Venice Beach Art" and click on images. Then you'll get a whole slew of ideas as well. For, if a picture is worth a thousand words then 10 pictures can probably make you ten thousand dollars at Venice Beach.

Sports Team(s)

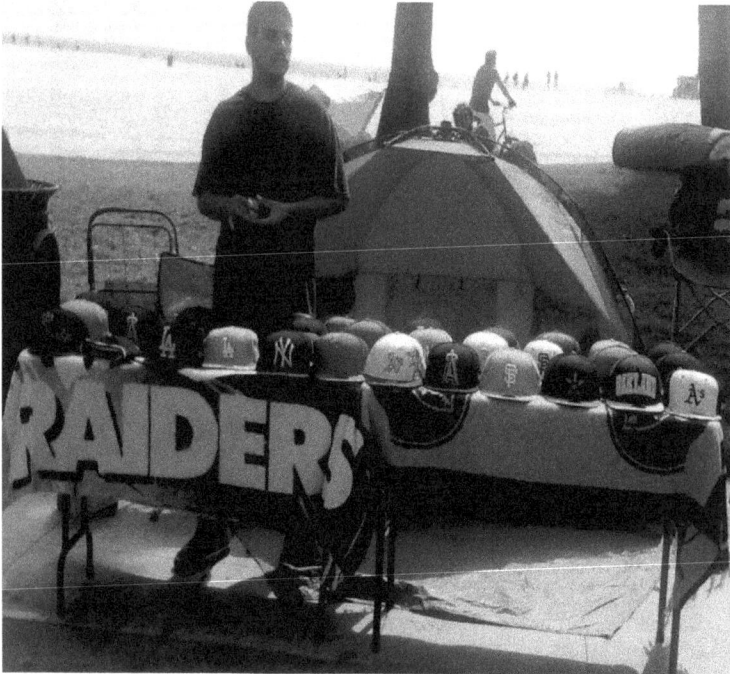

If there's one thing Los Angeles is known for it would definitely be the sports fanatics. From the Lakers to the Raiders and the Dodgers to the Kings, people love to buy things with LA Sports Teams on them. From Lakers cups, mugs, t-shirts and caps to Dodger pipes, umbrellas and necklaces, anything sports related is a winner. One person on Venice sells Marilyn Monroe in a Laker jersey and Einstein in a Dodger jacket, another sells every color LA Baseball cap you can think of, so it's totally up to you what you come up with. Venice is the one place that you don't have to worry about licensing, everybody bootlegs everything. So think it up, create it, buy it, sell it, and go hard in the paint. For, capitalism is an all season sport especially when selling anything dealing with sports.

99¢ STORE ANYTHING

Now, if all the things you've tried in the past have failed, there's one thing you can definitely do that is guaranteed to work and is basically a no-brainer; go to the "99¢ only" store. There are so many things in the 99¢ store you can flip into instant cash. A prime example is the "Doggy Store" on Venice Beach. The entire booth is made up of things for dogs (leashes, collars, water bowls, doggie treats—etc) and consists of items that sell for $5 but were purchased for 99¢. That's a 500% profit!!! All you need is a little creativity, drive and a few dollars. There are 99 ways at the 99¢ store to make a dollar (or 5 dollars) out of 99 cents.

VENDING FROM A TO Z
Things you can do or sell on the Boardwalk

A

Advice
African Soap

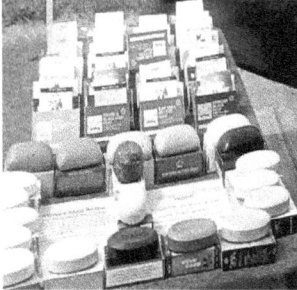

Animals (Live)

Animals (Stuffed)
Apples
Aprons
Art

Aluminum Airplanes

Angels

Avocados

B

Baby Clothes
Bags

Baked Goods

Balloons

Balls
Bandanas
Baseball Caps
Baseball Jerseys
Basketball Jerseys

Basketballs
Bath Salts

Batteries
Beach Balls
Beach Towels

Beads
Bells
Belly Button Rings
Belt Buckles

Belts
Beverages

Bibles
Bibs
Bicycles

Bikinis

Bill Folds
Bird Houses

Black Soap
Blankets
Blinds
Boats
Body Oils

94

Bongs

Boogie Boards
Books
Boomerangs
Booty Shorts
Bottles (For Incense)
Bowls
Bracelets

Braids
Bread
Bridal Gowns
Brims
Brooms
Brushes
Bum Signs

Bumper Stickers

Butterflies
Buttons

C

Cable Necklaces
Cake
Calendars
Cameras
Candles

Candy

Canes
Canvasses
Carved stones

Car Covers
Cards
Cars (Remote Control)
Cartoons
CD's

Children's C.D's

Cell phones
Cement Chalk
Characterization
Charms
Chess Sets
Chimes

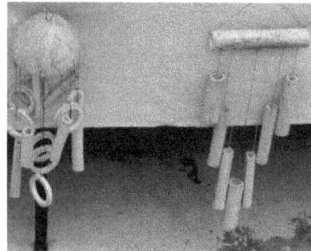

China
Chips
Chocolate
Chokers
Christ
Cigarettes
Cigars

Clocks

Clogs
Cloth (with Prints)

Colorful Clothing
Clowns
Coffee
Combs
Comedy
Comic Books
Cones (Incense)
Consciousness (Advice)
Cookies
Copper
Cork Screws
Corn on the Cob
Cosmetics
Costumes
Cotton

Crack
Cradles
Crafts
Cribs

Crocheted Caps
Crowns
Crystals

Cubes (Incense)
Culture
Curtains
Cymbals

D

Daisies
Dead Insects
Dental Products
Desserts
Diamonds
Diapers
Dice
Dips
Dishes

Dog Collars

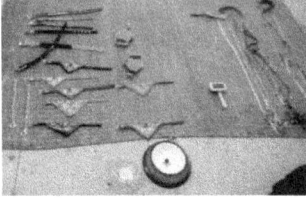

Dog Food
Dog Treats
Dogs

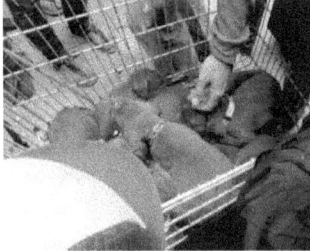

Dolls
Dominoes
Door Bells
Dresses
Dried Flowers
Drills
Drums

E

Eagles
Earmuffs
Earrings

Easels
Easter Eggs
Electric Bikes

Electric Skateboards

Elephants
Embroidery
Emeralds
Eyebrows
Eyeglasses

F

Fabric
Facepaint

Feathers

Feather Extensions

Films
Finger Nails
Fish
Fitness Apparel
Flags
Flowers

Flutes

Fortune Tellers

Fragrances

Framed Art

Fried Food

Frisbees
Frogs
Fruit

Funnel Cake

Fur Coats
Furniture

G

Games
Gift Boxes
Giraffes
Gliders
Glitter
Globes
Gloves
Goblets
God
Gold

Golf Accessories

Gongs
Gorillas
Gospel
Gourds
Grapes
Grasshoppers
Greeting Cards
Guitars
Gum

H

Hack Saw
Hackey Sacks

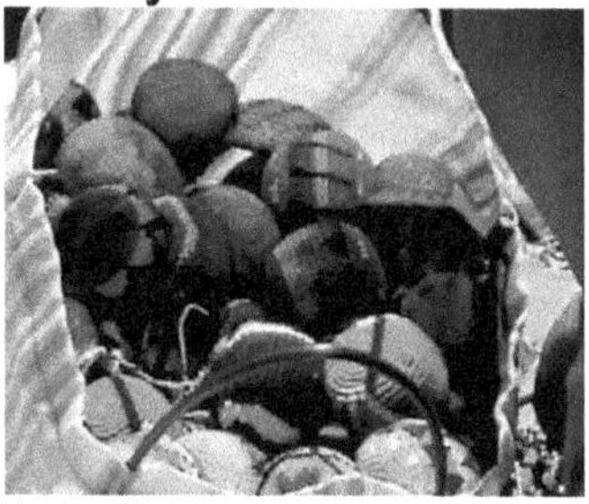

Hair Pieces
Haircuts
Handkerchiefs
Hangers
Harmonicas
Hats
Headbands
Headphones
Head wraps

Hearts
Helicopters
Helium
Henna Tattoos

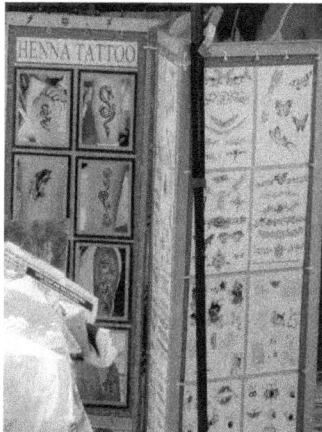

Herbs
Hieroglyphics
Highlighters
Hinduism Figures

Hip Hop

Hockey Jerseys
Holsters
Honeycombs
Hoodies
Hooks
Horoscopes

Horse Shoes
Hugs

Hula Hoops
Human Hair
Hunting Knives
Hydraulics
Hypnosis

I

Ice

Ice Cream (cart)
Illegal I.D.'s

Illustrations
Images
Indigenous Artifacts
Insects
Incense

Irie Gear

Iron Statues

Islam
Ivory

J

Jackets
Jade
Jam
Jars (Painted)
Jasmine (Incense)
Jazz (CDs & Art)

Jelly (Homemade)
Jelly Fish
Jerseys
Jets

Jewelry
Joints (Marijuana)
Jokes
Journals

Juggling

Juice
Jumpers

Junk

K

Kaleidoscopes
Karma
Keepsakes
Kelp
Ketchup (Homemade)
Key Chains

Keyboards
Khakis
Kick Drums
Kidney Beans (Canned)
Kilts
Kisses
Kites
Kittens
Kiwis
Knapsacks
Knives
Knowledge
Kosher Food

L

Ladders
Ladies (Paintings)

Ladles (Hand Painted)
Language Books
Lanterns
Latex (Condoms)
Laughter (Comedy)
Lavender (Oils & Incense)
Lawsuits
Leather Goods
Leaves (Dried & Matted)
Lectures (Live & CD's)

Ledgers
Leg Warmers
Lemon Cake

Lemonade
Lenses
Leopards
Leotards
Lessons
Lies
Lighthouses
Lighters

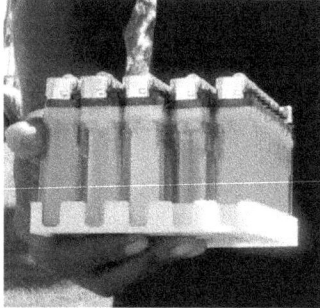

Limes
Linens
Lingerie

Lions (Stuffed)
Lip Gloss

Lips (Fake)
Lips (Tattoo)
Lipstick
Liquids
Literature
Lizards (Real & Fake)
Loaves of Bread
Lobsters
Locks
Logic
Lotion

Love

Luggage

Lumber
Lunches
Lyrics

M

Machetes (Plastic)
Machine Guns (Toy/Plastic)
Madonnas (Catholic)
Madonnas (Posters & T-shirts)
Magazines
Magic

Magnets
Magnifying Glasses
Mahogany
Make-up
Manicures
Mannequins
Mantillas
Maple Syrup
Maps

Marbles (Painted)
Marijuana

Marmalade (Homemade)
Marshmallows
Martial Arts
Marvel Comics
Masks
Massages

Matches
Material Cloth
Meaningful Metaphors
Medicines
Melons
Memorabilia

Menus
Merchandise
Mermaids

Mesh
Metal
Metaphysical Messages

Meteors
Meters
Mice
Microphones
Midgets

Miles Davis
Military (Badges, Costumes, Uniforms)
Milk

Mime

Minerals
Ministry
Mints
Mirrors
Mischief
Misogyny
Mists (Spray)
Mitts

Mixes (CD)
Mobile Phones
Mobsters (Posters)
Molasses
Money (Fake)

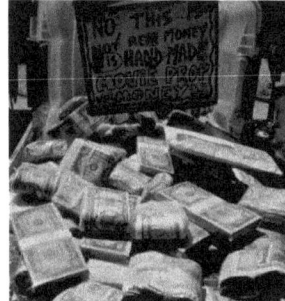

Monkeys (Stuffed)
Monks (Painting)
Monograms
Monopoly (Game)
Monsters
Moons (Toy & Painted)
Moose
Mops
Mormon (Literature)
Morphine
Mortal Combat (Video Game)
Moslem (Literature)
Mosque (Paintings)
Mosquitoes (Dead, Jewelry)
Mother's Day Cards
Moths (Dead)
Motion Pictures
Motorcycles (Parts,
Accessories, Paintings)
Mountains (Paintings)
Mouthpieces
Movies
Muffins
Muffs (Ear & Hand)
Mugs (Painted)

Mummies
Muscle Shirts

Mushrooms

Music (Live & Recorded)

Musk (Oil & Incense)
Muskets
Muslim (Literature)
Mustaches (Fake)
Mustard
Muzzles
Mysteries (Books & DVDs)
Mystical Merchandise
Mythology (Greek)

N

Naked Juice
Naked Paintings
**Names (on rice, on paper, in
sandstone on a painting)**

Napkins
Narcotics
Narrations (Storytellers)
National (Flags & Hats)
Native Americans (Paintings, Jewelry, T-shirts, Headdress and Dreamcatchers)

Natural Foods

Nature
Nautical
Navel Rings
Navy (Hats, Clothing, Badges, & Paintings)
Necklaces

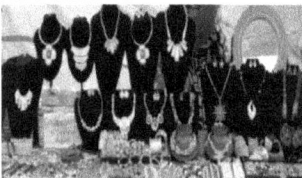

Neckties
Nectarines
Nectars
Negro League (Hats, Jerseys, Posters)
Neon (Paintings, Apparel)
Neptunes
Nestle Chocolate
Nests (Bird)
Nets
Nettles (Herb)
Newspapers
Nickle (Jewelry)
Nicotine (Cigarettes)
Night Lights
Night Sticks
Nightgowns
Nightshirts
Noises (Live, Recorded)
Nominal (Utility) Items
Nooses
Noses (Fake)
Notebooks
Notes
Nothing
Nudes (Paintings, Mannequins)
Nuggets (Gold & Marijuana)
Numbers (Painted)
Numerals
Nursery Books
Nutriment (Food)
Nutrition (Books, DVDs)
Nutritional Snacks
Nuts
Nylon (Apparel & Merchandise)
Nymphs (Artwork, Pictures)

O

Oars
Oatmeal
Obey (Clothing, Prints, Stickers)

Objects
Oboes
Occult (Paintings, Literature, Music)
Ocean (Seashells, Paintings, Recordings)

Octagons
Octopuses
Odds & Ends
Offensive Material
Official Merchandise
Ogres
Oils (Body, Burning)

Old School Merchandise
Olives
Omelettes
Onions
Onyx
Opera (Music)
Oranges
Orchestra (Music)
Orchids
Organic (Foods)
Organs (Instruments)
Oriental Foods
Ornaments
Oxygen (Oxygen Bar)
Oysters

P

Paddles
Padlocks
Pads (of Paper)
Pageant Crowns
Paint

Paintings
Pajamas

Palm Readings
Pamphlets
Pancakes

Panels
Panhandling
Panoramic Views
Pants
Paper
Parkas
Parrots
Paste
Patches

Patriotic (Buttons, Flags & T-shirts)

Patterns
Peaches
Peacocks
Peanuts
Pearls
Pears

Pebbles (Painted)
Pegs
Pencils
Penguins (Paintings)
Pens
Peppers
Percussion (Instruments)
Perfumes
Pets
Pharmaceuticals (Drugs)
Philosophy (Quotes and Paintings)

Phones

Photographs
Piano Lessons
Pianos
Pickles
Piercings
Pies
Piggy Banks
Pigs (Paintings)
Pillows

110

Pineapples
Pins
Pipes

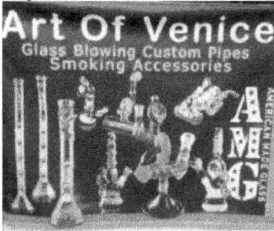

Pistols (Toys)
Pitchers
Planes (Toys& Paintings)

Planets (Paintings)
Plants
Plates (Painted)
Plays (Live performances)
Plugs
Plums
Pocketbooks

Poems (Framed & Recorded)
Poetry (Books & Live
Performances)

Politics

Pony (Tennis Shoes)
Pop (Soda)
Pop Stars(Music/Painted)
Pope (Paintings)

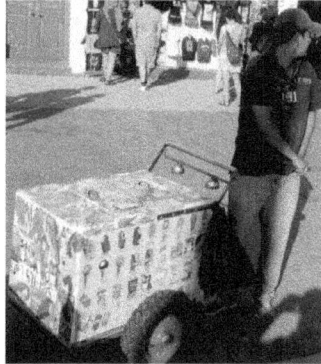

Popsicles
Porcelain
Pork
Pornography
Portfolios
Positive Thoughts

111

Postcards
Posters
Potatoes
Potions
Pots & Pans
Pottery
Powder
Pranks
Presidents (Photos, Paintings, T-shirts)

Pride Products (Homosexual)
Pride Products (Homosexual)

Prince (Music, Images)
Prints
Produce (Fruits & Vegetables)
Projectors
Prophecies
Prostitution
Protestant (Literature)
Psychic Readings

Publications
Pumpkin Pie

Puppets
Purses

112

Puzzles

Pyramids

Quotes

Q

Quartz
Queens (Drawings & Paintings)

Questions

R

Rabbits
Radios
Rafts
Rags
Railroad Trains
Rainbows (Drawn/Painted, Jewelry)
Rakes
Rapping (Live Performance & Recorded)

Ravens
Raw Food
Ray-Bans (Glasses)

Reality
Recipes
Records
Refrigerators
Religion

Restaurants

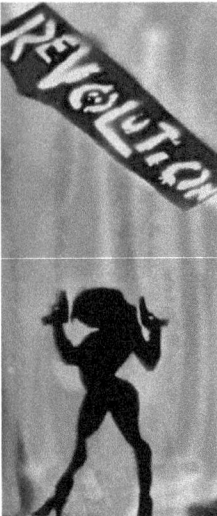

Revolution (Literature, Art, T-shirts)
Revolvers (Toys)
Rhymes
Rhythm
Ribbons
Ribs
Rice
Riddles

Rifles (Toy)
Rings

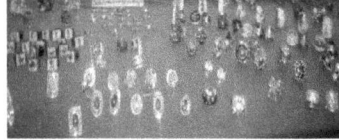

Robes (Rolls)
Robots
Rocks (Painted)
Romance (Cards, Art)
Roosters
Rose (Oil & Incense)
Roses
Rowboats
Rub (Massages)

Rubber bands
Rubies
Rulers
Rum

S

Sacks
Saddles
Safes
Sage

Sailboats
Sails
Saints (Painted)
Sandpaper
Salads
Sand Castles

Sandals

Sandwiches
Sanitary Napkins
Sapphires
Sarcasm
Satanic (Propaganda, Music & Art)
Satchels
Satellites
Saucers (Painted)
Sauces
Sausages
Saviors (Images, Literature)
Saws
Scales
Scallops
Scanners
Scarves

Scenery (Art)
Scents
Scepters
Scissors
Scoopers
Scopes
Scrabble (Game)
Scrambled Eggs
Screens (for pipes)
Screwdrivers
Scriptures (Art & Books)
Scrubs (Bathing & Shower scraps)
Scrubs (Medical Apparel)
Sculptures
Sea Salt
Seals
Seashells

Seasonings
Seeds
Sermons (Live Performances or Recorded)
Serpents
Servants
Sewing
Sex

Shades
Shakes
Shampoo
Sharks
Shaving Cream
Shea Butter

Sheets
Shields
Shimmery Jewelry
Shirts

Shoe Shine

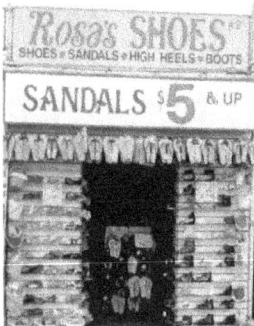

Shoes
Shorts
Shovels
Shower Caps
Silver

Sincerity
Singing
Skateboards

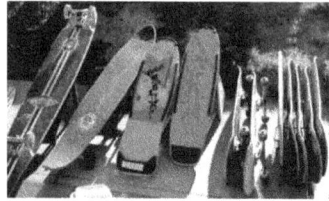

Skeletons
Sketches
Skillets
Skis
Skulls

Slavery (Artifacts & Photos)
Slippers
Slogans
Slurpees
Slushies
Smoothies
Smothered Potatoes
Snacks
Snails
Snakes
Snickers
Snoop Dogg
Socialism (Literature)
Socks
Soda
Songs
Sorcery (Images & Literature)
Soul

116

Sounds (Music)
Speeches (Live Performances
& Recorded)
Spices (Seasoning)

**Spiritual (T-shirts, Art,
Music, Clothing, Literature)**
Spoken Words
Sponges
Spools (Thread)
Spoons
Sports (Images & Apparel)
Spread (Sandwich)
Sprint (Phones, Earpieces)
Spring Rolls
Sprouts
Spurs
Squares (Cigarettes)
Squares (Painted)
Squashes
Squeezed Juice (Fresh)
Squirt (Drink)
Squirt Guns
Stallions
Stamps (Collectible)

Staples
Stars
Stationery
Statues
Steak
Steamed Vegetables
Stenography
Sticks (for Walking)
Stilts
Stockings
Stones (Painted)
Stools
Stoves (Camping)
Strings (Guitar)
Subscriptions (Magazine)
Subway (Sandwiches)
Sugar
Suits
Sun-dried Tomatoes
Sunglasses

Supper
Surfboards

Surveys
Sweatpants
Sweatshirts
Sweatsuits
Swimmer's Trunks
Swine
Swords

Syringes
Syrups

T

T.V. (Performance)

T.V.'s
Table
Tablespoons
Tackle (Fishing)
Tags (Clothing)
Tags (Graffiti)
Tailoring
Tails (Real & Fake)
Talent (Performances)
Tangerines
Tap Dancing
Tape
Tapes (Mixed Audio)
Targets
Tarts (Food)
Tassels

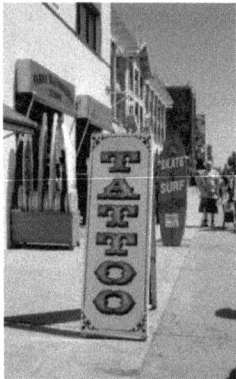

Tattoos

Taxi Rides
Teams (Sports)
Teas
Teaspoons
Technology
Teeth (Animals)
Teeth (Plastic, Rubber, Fake & Gold Plated)
Telegrams (Singing)
Telepathy (Psychic)
Telephones
Temples (Literature & Photos)
Temporary Tattoos (Henna)

Tennis Balls
Tennis Rackets
Tennis Shoes
Textiles
Theatre (Performance)
Theology (Literature)
Thermal Clothing
Thermometers
Thermostats
Thinking
Thoughts
Tickets (Concerts)
Ties (for Suits)
Tiles (Painted)
Tin
Toads
Toast
Tobacco
Toboggans
Toddler's Clothes

Toilet Tissue
Toilets (Painted)
Tomahawks
Tongs
Tongues (Fake)
Tonics
Topography
Torches
Torpedos (Toy & Photos)
Tortoises
Tote Bags

Towels (Beach Towels)

Towers (Art)
Tractors (Toy)
Trademarks (Drawn)
Trailers (Bikes)
Trainers (Gym)
Transients (Panhandling)
Transistors
Transmissions (Auto Mechanics)
Travel (Agents)
Trays (Painted)

Treasure Chests

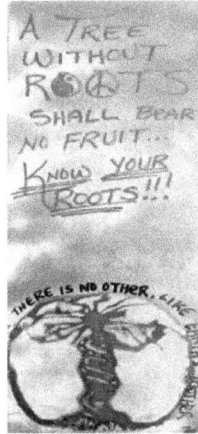

Trees (Real, Fake, Painted)
Tricks (Magic)
Trophies
Trunks
Truth
Tubas
Tubes
Tubs
Tugboats
Tumblers
Turbans
Turquoise
Turtles
Tweed
Tweezers
Typing

U

Ukuleles
Ultraviolet Lamps
Umbrellas
Umpire's Outfits
Underground Music
Underworld Figures

Unicorn

Uniforms
Unity
Universe (Paintings)

Universities (Shirts, Hats, Buttons)
Utensils (Kitchen, Cooking, Writing, Painting)
Utopia (Images, Phrases)

V

Vagabonds (Panhandling)
Vaginas (Rubber, Paintings, Portraits)
Vagrants (Panhandling)
Vases (Painted)
Veal
Vegetables
Vehicles
Velvet
Venus (Painted)
Verses (Performance)
Videos
Villains (Painted, T-shirts)
Vinegar

Vinyl (Records)
Viola
Violets
Violins
Virgin Mary (Paintings, Jewelry, T-shirts)
Visors
Vitamins

W

Wafers
Waffles
Wagons
Walkers (Elderly)
Wallets
Walnuts
Walruses (Stuffed & Paintings)
Waltz (CD's)
Wardrobes

Watches

Water
Weapons
Weasels
Weaves
Weed
Whales
Wheat
Whiskey
Whistles
Wigs
Wind Chimes

Windmills (miniature)
Windpipes
Windshield Wipers
Wine
Wings (Angel)
Winter Hats
Wire Art
Wire Jewelry

Wisdom (Advice)
Wishes (Psychic)
Witches (Toy & Paintings)
Wives (Marriages)
Wizards (Performances & Painted)
Wolves (Toy & Paintings)
Wonder Woman (Dolls, Paintings, T-shirts)
Wood Burnt Art

Wood Carvings
Wood Frames
Wooden Jewelry

Wooden Pipes

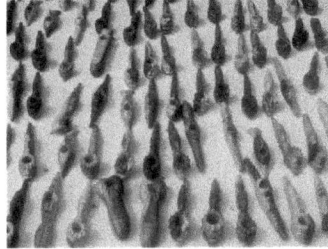

Wool (Clothing, Hats)
Words (Performance, Poetry, Phrases, T-shirts, Art, etc)
Worlds (Toy, Mini Globes, Painted)
Worms (Gummy, Candy, Toy/Rubber)
Worn (Clothes)
Wraps (Food)
Wraps (Head Wraps)
Wrenches
Wristbands

Writings (Poetry)
Written Material (Literature)

X

Xylophones (Miniature, Toys)

121

Y

Yachts (Toy-Remote Control, Paintings)
Yams
Yankees (Hats, T-shirts, Mugs)
Yardsticks
Yarn
Yearly Calendars
Yellow Jackets (Bees, Drawings)
Yews (Picture/Paintings)
Yodeling (Performance)
Yoga (Mats, Paintings, DVD's, Apparel)

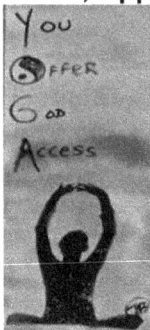

Yogurt
Youth (Anti-Aging crèmes, Herbs)
Youth (Children selling/vending)

Yuccas (Paintings, Drawings)

Z

Zebras (Toy, Stuffed, Paintings)
Zeitgeist (DVD's)

Zen (Buddhas, Jewelry, Paintings)
Zepplin (Led Zepplin Music, Posters, T-shirts)
Zig-zags (Rolling Papers)
Zinc (Herb/Vitamins)
Zinnia (Paintings)
Zithers (Handmade, Miniature)
Zodiac (Psychic Readings, Astrological)
Zombies (Stuffed, Paintings)
Zoo (Paintings & Stuffed Animals)
Zucchinis

RESOURCE GUIDE

Art Stores

Aaron Brothers
1645 Lincoln Boulevard
Santa Monica, CA 90404-3711
(310) 450-6333

13455 Maxella Avenue Ste. 250
Marina Del Rey, CA 90292-5684
(310) 577-1040

www.aaronbrothers.com

Blick (Art Stores)
11531 Santa Monica Boulevard
West Los Angeles, CA 90025
(310) 479-1416

www.dickblick.com

*Great assortment of pens, brushes, etc.

Michael's
1427 Fourth Street
Santa Monica, CA 90401-2308
(310) 393-9634

www.michaels.com

*Great for frames, canvas, stencils, pens or anything artistic…and always has sales.

The Party Store
2480 S. Sepulveda Boulevard
Los Angeles, CA 90064
(310) 312-6050

www.partycity.com

*The best place for balloons and a clown costume or props for kids for performances.

Utrecht
11677 Santa Monica Boulevard
Los Angeles, CA 90025
(310) 478-5755

www.utrechtart.com

*The best deals on canvases hands down. The employees are artists and frequent Venice often. They sell everything you would need at a discount that beats all the rest of the art stores.

99¢ Only Stores
241 Lincoln Boulevard
Venice, CA 90291
(310) 393-9634

www.99only.com

*99¢ store has a "Club 99¢" membership where you can buy online and ship to the store you need them at.

Bob Marley/Rasta Merchandise

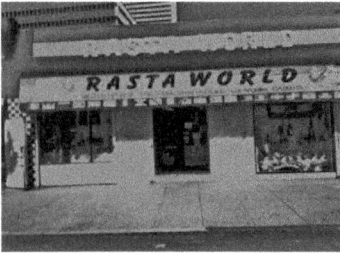

Rasta World
1135 S. Main Street
Los Angeles, CA 90015
(213) 747-2216

*Bob Marley and African, Jamaican, Caribbean, Rasta flags, wristbands, necklaces, bracelets, belts, purses, jerseys, dresses, earrings, etc.

Costco

13463 Washington Boulevard
Marina Del Rey, CA 90292
(310) 754-2003

www.costco.com

Mon-Fri 11:00 AM – 8:30 PM
Sat   9:30 AM – 6:00 PM
Sun   10:00 AM – 6:00 PM

Feathers

Royal Trading Company
1133 ½ S. Main Street
Los Angeles, CA 90015
(213) 746-8252

*$6/one dozen multiple colors and styles.

Hat/Caps

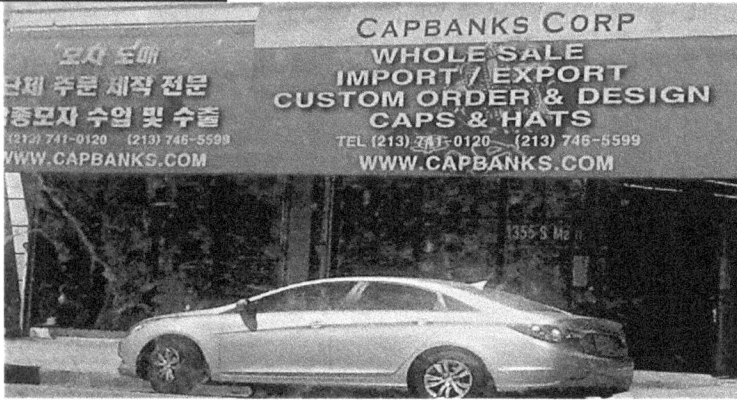

Capbanks
1355 S. Main Street
Los Angeles, CA 90015
(213) 741-0120

www.capbanks.com

Santo Cap
1317 S. Main Street Ste. A
Los Angeles, CA 90015
(213) 749-2277

Hip Hop Jewelry

Eureka Traders
430 S. Los Angeles Street #5
Los Angeles, CA 90013
(213) 622-4514

*Belt buckles, the Bling Bling wholesale shop.

Jewelry

Daniel
1137 S. Main Street
Los Angeles, CA 90015
(213) 749-8720

*Specializes in products for the hair for kids and cosmetics.

Royal Trading Company
1133 ½ S. Main Street
Los Angeles, CA 90015
(213) 746-8252

*Specializes in bracelets, necklaces, feathers, earrings and scarves.

Trans Co.
1133 S. Main Street
Los Angeles, CA 90015

*Keychains, earrings, hats or anything from China.

Music Instruments & Amplifiers

Guitar Center
10831 W. Pico Boulevard
Los Angeles, CA 90064
(310) 475-0637

www.guitarcenter.com

Mon-Fri 10:00 AM – 9:00 PM
Sat   10:00 AM – 8:00 PM
Sun   11:00 AM – 7:00 PM

Sam Ash
7360 Sunset Boulevard
Los Angeles, CA 90046-3487
(323) 850-1050

www.samash.com / www.samashmusic.com

Mon-Fri 10:00 AM – 9:00 PM
Sat   10:00 AM – 8:00 PM
Sun   11:00 AM – 7:00 PM

*Roland Street Cube/Street Amp Series run on "AA" batteries...perfect for performances at Venice.

Paint/Hardware

Home Depot
12975 W. Jefferson Boulevard
Los Angeles, CA 90066
(310) 822-3330

www.homedepot.com

Mon-Fri 5:00 AM – 12:00 PM
Sat/Sun 6:00 AM – 11:00 PM

*Wood (for frames), spray paint, rugs, tents, tables, everything needed to be a profitable vendor at Venice Beach.

Osh (Orchard Supply Hardware)
2020 Bundy Drive
West Los Angeles, CA 90025
(310) 571-3838

www.osh.com

Mon-Fri 7:00 AM – 9:00 PM
Sat/Sun 8:00 AM – 8:00 PM

*Spray paint (1.99-3.00), great customer service.

Printing

Dynamic Image
909 Ocean Front Walk
Venice, CA 90291
(310) 399-7667

Mon-Fri 9:00 AM – 5:00 PM

*The best place for copying and printing of posters and lithographs
any size, full color or black and white.

Staples Copy and Print Shop
2570 Lincoln Boulevard Ste 103
Venice, CA 90291
(310) 306-2720

Mon-Thurs 7:00 AM – 9:00 PM
Fri   9:00 AM – 7:00 PM
Sat/Sun   10:00 AM – 6:00 PM

1501 Lincoln Boulevard
Venice, CA 90291
(310) 577-6740

Mon-Thurs 8:00 AM – 9:00 PM
Fri   9:00 AM – 7:00 PM
Sat/Sun   10:00 AM – 6:00 PM

*Great place for printing, pens, glue, electronics, arts, crafts, etc.

Purses/Handbags

Lauren Hand Bag
1120 S. Main Street
Los Angeles, CA 90015
(213) 746-8854/9491

*Upscale designer bags.

Sense
1114 ½ S. Main Street
Los Angeles, CA 90015

*Children's backpacks Dora, Hello Kitty, Barbie, Sponge Bob, etc.

*On Main Street (at 12th) there are 15 to 20 shops that carry over 500-1000 products, backpacks, etc. that you can easily resale for a profit. No ID, no reseller's permit, nor business license is required. Most don't take credit, only hard (under the table) cash. Here are a few of them:

Pro Vision Sunglasses
1157 S. Main Street
Los Angeles, CA 90015
(213) 748-0383

S. H. Handbags, Luggage, Backpacks
1155 S. Main Street
Los Angeles, CA 90015
(213) 744-1155

Seashells & Beach Accessories

www.shellshopping.com
www.seashellco.com
www.atlanticcoralenterprise.com
www.shellhorizons.com

*You can set up the perfect seaside booth simply by ordering from these online companies.

Sports

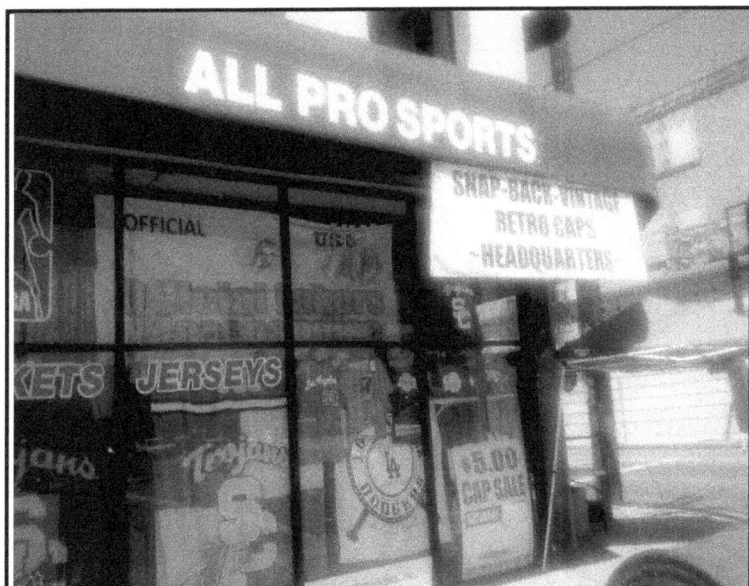

All Pro Sports
1601 S. Main Street
Los Angeles, CA 90015
(213) 743-9100

*Wholesale anything sports team related – hats, towels, jerseys, etc.

Deportes Si Se Puede
1325 S. Main Street
Los Angeles, CA 90015
(213) 747-2751
*Soccer, football jerseys, balls, etc.

T-Shirts

Sun Active
1750 S. Main Street
Los Angeles, CA 90015
(213) 743-9350

Conclusion

If you live in Southern California, there is no excuse for poverty unless you are disabled, elderly, sick or mentally retarded. Between Hollywood and Downtown LA (the Wholesale District), there lies a multitude of opportunities for wealth if you are willing to get up, get out and get them. Even if you live in the hood and are in extreme poverty, there are riches and fame that can be accessed just by jumping on a bus or a metro rail and changing your scenery and attitude.

You are the master of your own destiny. *You are co-creating your reality just by thinking whatever thoughts you choose. If you want to win, visualize yourself winning. If you want wealth and abundance, picture yourself without a need. See yourself with everything your heart desires and imagine riches, health and happiness as yours everyday*. ***That's the beautiful thing about your mind. It is completely yours and you can use it any way you choose to***. It's your oyster you can open it and see the pearls that lie before you.

If you have this book in your hands or are reading it online, you have already made a conscious choice to be at the greatest beach on Earth and to become the greatest you that you can be.

What makes Venice the greatest beach is not so much the sand and beach itself, but the freedom and flexibility you have while on it. It's the artistic liberty and political expressive leniency that no other seashore in the world can boast. *You have a million ways to become successful, comfortable and stable on the Boardwalk.* But you must define what success means to you, close your eyes, sit in silence, visualize yourself being there and then affirm it mentally. What does it feel like, sound like, look like and taste like? What does it make you act like, talk like, walk like and live like?

When you answer these questions, then you will know what you must start seeing and being right now. If you do this, the universe will do the rest and then…it shall be.

So, read this *Money Manual"* and *Metaphysical Map"* again and again and then…memorize it, visualize it and implement it…and I'll see you at the beach!!!

Additional Info

In compliance with the laws of the State of California, **I must give these contacts**. If, when and how you use them is completely up to you.

IRS (Internal Revenue Services)
300 N. Los Angeles Street #4
Los Angeles, CA 90012-3313
(213) 576-3009

The State of California Board of Equalization
PO Box 942879
Sacramento, CA 94279-0001
Culver City District (310) 342-1000
www.boe.ca.gov

Purpose: Register business and pay State Taxes

Los Angeles Business License Commission
500 W. Temple Street
Los Angeles, CA 90012-2713
(213) 974-7691
www.lacity.org / www.losangelesworks.org

Purpose: To obtain LA City Business License

LA County Treasurer and Tax Collector
http://ttc.lacounty.gov

LA County Department of Social Services
2707 Grand Avenue
Los Angeles, CA 90007
(866) 613-3777
www.foodstampsnetwork.net/ebt-card
www.ladpss.org

Purpose: To obtain Welfare (Food Stamps, Housing, Money)

Unemployment Benefits
(877) 238-9373
www.edd.ca.gov
www.california.edd.ca.gov

City of Los Angeles Department of Recreation and Parks
Venice Beach Recreation Center
(310) 396-6764

ACKNOWLEDGEMENTS

I must first give thanks and praise to the **CREATOR** called a many names in a many languages and praised, acknowledged, worshipped, and appreciated in a multitude of ways each and every day. For, without that universal, metaphysical, cosmic energy, I would not be able to function nor have the motivation to be the being that I am.

Secondly, I must give thanks to my **queen mother**, Myna Brown, my father Clyde Wells and my sisters Colene and Latasha. Thank you for believing in me when no one would nor could. It's for you that I've done all that I've done thus far.

Thirdly, I give thanks and all the credit to my son Heru. This is so he will always remember that his daddy did good things and was a good man.

Special thanks goes out to:

Venice Beach Walking Tours www.venicebeachwalkingtours.com

Westland Network www.westland.net

Venice Historical Society www.venicehistorical.org

Venice Centennial www.virtualvenice.info

Free Venice Beachhead www.freevenice.org

LA CITY NEWS www.lacitynews.blogspot.com

LA Curbed www.LA.curbed.com

LA Times www.latimes.com

Spirit Of Venice www.spiritofvenice.wordpress.com

Spirit Of Venice www.spiritofvenice.net

Venice 311 www.venice311.org

Yo Venice www.yovenice.com

Name On Rice www.nameonrice.com

Venice Paparazzi www.venicecpaparazzi.com

Big Daddy's Pizza, Ocean Blue, Fruit Gallery,
Mao's Kitchen, All American Burger
The Bistro, The Sidewalk Café', Dynamic Image

And my folks...

Ra Ra Superstarr
Damon Warren
Kwanzaa
Vivian
Jean Paul
Smell Good
Marky Mark (Wal Mark)
Carlos
Dennis from Venice
Matt Dowd
Kenny
Mike Hunt
Bear
Jingles
Fluent
Juan
Stacy
Jason
And...

Everyone else at Venice Beach that continues to hustle, grind, dream and work hard to become a success!!!
Just do IT!!!

ABOUT THE AUTHOR:

Tony B. Conscious

Hip-Hop / Funk / Rock / Soul / Spoken Word Artist

A renaissance man (Harlem Renaissance that is),
TONY B. CONSCIOUS
is the personification of *AFRICAN-AMERICAN* culture.

He is (amongst other things) A **B-BOY, BEATBOX,EMCEE, GRAFFITI/VISUAL ARTIST (known as "THE GHETTO VAN-GO"), Poet/ Spoken Word Artist, Vocalist, AUTHOR, ACTIVIST, VEGAN VEGETARIAN and PHILOSOPHER.**

AS a member of **THE UNIVERSAL ZULU NATION, THE TEMPLE OF HIP HOP** and **AGAPE INTERNATIONAL SPIRITUAL CENTER,** he seeks to use each and every element of HIP HOP to inspire, educate , motivate and redirect the inner-city youth and the HIP HOP COMMUNITIES WORLDWIDE to a place of balance, harmony, creativity, PEACE & LOVE.

He has not only worked for the **OBAMA** campaign (coined —ℝe Obama Hip Hop Hype Man"), he has also been on stage and on tour with **KRS-ONE, GRANDMASTER FLASH, KOOL HERC, BUSY BEE, PUBLIC ENEMY, KOOL MO DEE, GRANDMASTER CAZ, PARIS, TUPAC and ERYKAH BADU** just to name a few.

HE is and will be, until he passes on to the next dimension, truly the personification of **HIP HOP, Poetry, Funk & Soul** music.

DISCOGRAPHY:

DIARY OF A BLAKMAN.	(1998)	SPOKEN WORD C.D.
ESCAPE FROM L.A.	(1999)	SPOKEN WORD C.D.
UNPLUGGED	(2002)	SPOKEN WORD C.D
(LIVE & UNCENSORED)	(2003)	SPOKEN WORD C.D.
P.O.E.T.	(2005)	SPOKEN /HIP HOP
A PICTURE'S WORTH	(2006)	SPOKEN WORD C.D.
FREE THE JENA 6	(2007)	HIP HOP SINGLE
KATRINA vs. WILLIE LYNCH	(2007)	HIP HOP SINGLE
I BARACK THE MIC RIGHT	(2008)	HIP HOP/RAP C.D
A.G.A.P.E	(2009)	HIP HOP/ GOSPEL
ELV8TE	(2009)	HIP HOP /FUNK
HELP HAITI	(2010)	HIP HOP SINGLE

BOOKS:

DIARY OF A BLACKMAN	(1998)	POETRY
BLACK HISTORY 101	(1999)	POETRY
100% NATURAL	(1999)	POETRY
BLACK LOVE	(1999)	POETRY
HUEMANITY	(1999)	POETRY
SPIRIT INSIDE	(2000)	POETRY
MASTERPIECES	(2002)	POETRY
A PICTURE'S WORTH...	(2006)	POETRY/ART
LIFE'S A BEACH (& then U die)	(2011)	Autobiography
How to Vend And Win !!!	(2011)	Instruct. Manual
* More Than Just Words...	(2011)	Acronyms
* (Always Resonating Truth)	(2011)	Art
* Do u Understand the words?	(2011)	Quotes

(Still in the process of publishing)

MERCHANDISE:

CONSCIOUS ENTERPRISES   *(1998)* *Political Apparel*
Fly Dye Art   *(2002)* *Visual Art /Merch.*
Barack Is Beautiful   *(2008)* *Obama Merch.*

For bookings, products
or other info:

CONSCIOUS ENTERPRISES/
FLY DYE ART
c/o ANTHONY BROWN (TONY B. CONSCIOUS)
PO Box 75882 la, ca 90075   **Cell: (323)251-4969**

EMAIL(S): fly_dye@hotmail.com   art info
        Flydye_art@hotmail.com   Art shows
        B_conscious@hotmail.com   Music, Poetry
        Teamobama@hotmail.com   Obama/political
        Flydyeart@gmail.com   International info

* ALL E-MAIL INQUIRIES WILL BE ANSWERED PROMPTLY.

ONLINE SITES & LINKS

Personal WEBSITES:

www.tonybconscious.com

www.flydye.com

www.flydyeart.com

www.poetrygear.com

www.beautifulbarack.com

Social Networks / Online Stores:

www.facebook.com/tonybconscious1

www.facebook.com/tonybconscious2

www.twitter.com/B_conscious

www.myspace.com/tonybconscious

www.myspace.com/flydye

www.youtube.com/tonybconscious

www.tunecore.com/music/tonybconscious

www.ourstage.com/fanclub/tonybconscious

www.elevatepresents.com/profile/TONYBCONSCIOUS

www.reverbnation.com/tonybconscious

www.modelrun.com/actor/tonybconscious

www.nextcat.com/tonybconscious

http://venice311.org/venice-boardwalk/boardwalk-vendors-artists-performers/venice-beach-artist-performer-activist-directory/tony-b-conscious/

KEEP IN TOUCH !!!
TONY B. CONSCIOUS

www.ingramcontent.com/pod-product-compliance
Lightning Source LLC
Chambersburg PA
CBHW030842210326
41521CB00025B/700